# Tales From Death Row

S J Parker

Published by SJP Publishing, 2023.

While every precaution has been taken in the preparation of this book, the publisher assumes no responsibility for errors or omissions, or for damages resulting from the use of the information contained herein.

TALES FROM DEATH ROW

**First edition. August 10, 2023.**

Copyright © 2023 S J Parker.

ISBN: 979-8223107453

Written by S J Parker.

# Table of Contents

*For Vicki, my heart, my soulmate,*

*Always*

# An Introduction from the Author

First, thank you for buying my collection and supporting a Death Row artist. I started writing without the intent of ever publishing my work in this fashion, but, as is often the case, life will take you on the most unexpected of journeys.

My hope and goal is to share with you some of my life, thoughts and experiences since being sent to Death Row. What people call the 'prison experience' can't truly be understood by anyone on the outside looking in, so I hope you will get an inkling of what I and the rest of Death Row goes through. That being said, I also don't want to minimize the hardships of what the family, friends and loved ones of someone in prison or Death Row go through. Without your love, support and friendship, I know that a terrible situation can get infinitely worse, so thank you.

I arranged my collection in chronological order so that you can glimpse my own personal journey from incarceration to present day. My early writings are a bit maudlin, if I'm being honest, and deal with the emotional trauma I suffered through and how I coped with it. I found writing about it to be very therapeutic with the added benefit of reminding myself of what is truly important in my life, such as it is. Later, my writing became a tool to express my thoughts and feelings on events that directly affected my 'prison experience'. I often view it like the exorcizing of a demon or lancing of a boil as I address issues related to mental health and incarceration in general. Many of these were written while I was in solitary confinement, which was how Death Row inmates were housed until 2017. After that, a lawsuit got us out of solitary confinement and into a much less isolated, more social setting and the tenor of my writing changed dramatically.

These later writings illustrate a lot more of my humor and the unique way I can see things. Not so coincidentally, this change in my writing style coincided with me meeting the love of my life and soul mate, Vicki, who would later become my wife. There is a wonder to finding something as precious to me as our relationship while I'm in the worst of circumstances and I am eternally grateful that I did. We've supported each other through difficult and heartbreaking times and come out stronger for the experience. None of this is possible without her.

So, I hope you enjoy my essays, anecdotes and poetry (actually, I'm not a poet, just a writer who has written a few poems, so temper your expectations appropriately) and thank you once again for supporting this collection, it means the world to me. Also, a shout out and big thank you to my son, Matthew, who did the cover art for this collection. I'm not sure where he got his artistic talent, but it wasn't from me. Well done, Matt!

Finally, I want to thank my parents, children, friends and family, both stateside and across the Pond, as you all are my strength and purpose to continue my struggle for a brighter future. I love you all.

# Labyrinth

"I didn't start really writing about my feelings of being on Death Row until almost three years after I was sentenced. Personally, it was a very dark time both mentally and emotionally and took a while for me to articulate those thoughts and feelings. Turns out that my struggles weren't uncommon to those in my situation, something I discovered as I began to talk and get to know my peers. This knowledge helped me write this short essay which I entered in a writing competition. It won first place, but, for me, the real prize was discovering an outlet to truly express myself in a constructive, meaningful way. It's my first ever published story and one of my favourites."

· · · ·

Prison can change a person in a multitude of ways. It can erode away our spirit and smother our dreams, alter our perceptions and deceive our minds. But the thing many fear the most is that we will be so irrevocably changed, that we will, for all intents and purposes, become lost, that some fundamental aspect of who we are and what defines us will have been ripped away forever.

If life in prison were likened to that of a Greek tragedy, it could easily be that of the story of the hero, Theseus, the dreaded Minotaur and Daedalus' Labyrinth. In prison, though you are locked in a cell, you can become lost in a Labyrinth of your own making. Your mind can warp your sense of reality, your sense of self, until you are hopelessly changed as to be unrecognizable to everyone, including yourself. You may desire to navigate this mental, emotional maze back to your true self, but none of us are Theseus, in possession of Ariadne's string to magically lead us out of the Labyrinth to freedom. Instead, we are alone, at the mercy of dark thoughts and twisted emotions that can lead us down even darker corridors within ourselves.

Our monsters, our own personal Minotaur's, if you will, can be very real to us, lurking around the corner, stalking us, ready to devour us whole. These monsters can be our anger at our circumstances, at the world or even at ourselves. They can be our despair and frustration with life or the legal system. They can be anything and everything that leads us astray from ourselves. If you aren't vigilant of your own self-awareness, you may find that the person in your cell, living in your skin, is a stranger, the former occupant a distant memory, another victim to our own personal variation of Daedalus' Labyrinth.

Yet, with even so grim a depiction of the pitfalls to incarceration, there is still the chance of salvation. It can come in ways both expected and unexpected. Every time our family and friends visit or send us a letter demonstrating their unconditional love and support, we are led back to another piece of ourselves. Every smile from our children reminds us that the best part of us will, in some way, endure beyond whatever existence fate has bestowed upon us. Every time a stranger reaches out to us, willing to befriend a convict in the direst of circumstances with something as simple as a kind word or an offer of friendship, it can invigorate our sense of self-worth. For us, these are our own magical strings, helping us to escape our Labyrinth with the greatest of gifts. The one gift that, if we are blessed with it, can sustain us in the present and in our futures. The one gift that, when nurtured, can never be lost or taken away. The one gift that will always help us remember ourselves. That one gift is hope.

"This essay was demonstrative of how different prison life is compared to 'civilian' life. It was eye opening for me, someone who'd never been to prison before, to enter such a strange social environment that was so vastly different from the one I was used to."

· · · ·

Prison can be a funny place. Not funny in a 'ha-ha' way, but funny in a weird way. It's a mixture of bald truths and contradictions that can baffle the mind while making perfect sense.

First, you are arrested for breaking the law. After being put on trial, where you have the opportunity to defend yourself, you are judged by a jury of your peers. If found innocent, you return to society. If found guilty, you go to prison, leaving behind the world you know for a newer and far more hazardous one. It's a world with a whole new set of rules and standards of behaviour, where one false step can unwittingly lead you down an irrevocable path to animosity, conflict and, in some cases, danger.

It's almost like your first day of school. You know nothing about your schoolmates, and they know nothing of you. At lunch, you are surrounded by strangers and never feel more alone. You are leery of talking to the wrong person lest they aren't part of the 'cool crowd'. Once you decide what to do, in many ways, your fate is sealed because this will be the first thing you are known for, the first impression you make to the people you will be surrounded by and interact with.

During class, under the watchful eyes of your teachers, you behave, follow the rules because if you don't, you get detention. At recess, however, when there are no teachers, a whole new set of rules are in effect: Playground Rules. Everyone separates into their own cliques. Sometimes they are divided by race, sometimes by neighbourhood, but, most often, it's by social standing. You aren't allowed to mix with others and if you break any of the unwritten rules, you risk being shunned and cast out of your chosen clique, forever a pariah that can lead to petty grudges and confrontations.

Prison casts an eerie reflection of this school and its playground. There are guards instead of teachers, solitary confinement instead of detention and a prison recreation yard instead of a playground. The cliques fall along race lines with each breaking down even further into their own individual sub-cliques that can be hopelessly complicated while making perfect sense to the career convict. Talk to the wrong person, hang out with the wrong race, attach yourself to the wrong side of an issue and your reputation is forever blackened, never to recover. But it can have further repercussions in the form of a surprise beating or even a metal shank.

One of the ironies of prison is that, for a collection of people thrown together for breaking the rules, prison has its own set of rules you have to follow. However, unlike how the saying goes, these rules aren't meant to be broken. To get along, you have to go along, to follow these new Playground Rules.

"I have twin children who have had to grow up while I've been here. They are adults now and about to start college, but my lasting memory of them was when they were barely six months old, and it sustains me to this day."

• • • •

They say that Death Row is simply a place where you wait to die.

They call us the Condemned. With that kind of endorsement, the motivation to get off my rack every day can be elusive. I mean, seriously, what's the point? Why bother caring?

This is the dilemma I struggle with again and again, day after day. But there is one thing that keeps me going. It's a memory, an ideal, the light at the end of the tunnel, if you will.

It's after midnight when the twins' crying wakes me up. Slipping out of bed, I pad down the hallway to the nursery, pushing open the door.

Of the two, Azia is louder, chubby fists waving as she screams with lusty vigour. Matthew, on the other hand, is whimpering quietly, upset at having been unceremoniously roused by his sister.

Scooping Azia out of her crib, I pat her bottom. She needs a change and a bottle before she'll be able to get back to sleep. I peel off the soiled diaper, using a baby wipe and powder before fastening on a fresh one. She stops crying as soon as I pick her up again. Staring at me with her hazel eyes, she gives me a smile so sweet, it makes my stomach clench. I hitch her up to my shoulder and her arms wrap around my neck to squeeze tight. I coo and bounce her on my way to the kitchen and I'm rewarded with a delighted giggle.

I prepare two bottles for my children and Azia is sucking greedily on hers while I carry her back to the nursery. Matthew has stopped sniffling and his brown eyes follow me as I tuck Azia back in. When his gaze locks onto the second bottle, his face lights up, tiny hands straining upward.

He all but snatches it from my grasp. Soon, the sound of my children feeding fills the room.

I stand between their cribs, shifting my attention from one to the other. Just looking at them causes me to smile and my heart to swell. But even as they work on their bottles, their eyes are focused on me, watching me as I watch them. There is no guile or artifice in their expressions, only the innocence and trust a six-month-old can possess. It says, 'I see you. I know you. And I love you.'

The memory of seeing those looks of trust and unconditional love is what still moves me to my very soul. The hope that is created when I relive that memory is what helps me get up every day. Because for me, one of the Condemned, what else could possibly inspire me to carry on, to endure, if not for this hope, this quality of love.

# Cage and Wheel

"I've never considered myself a poet, but sometimes an idea or feeling just can't be expressed any other way."

• • • •

Trapped in this sombre cage of steel,
    My legs churning on this hamster's wheel.
    The days are endless, full of doubt,
    When will it stop, will I ever get out?
    I can feel the ghosts of inmate's past,
    Their pain, their sorrow, their futile wrath.
    I fear to join this legion of shades,
    Screaming to heaven, as my soul fades.
    Can I escape, this cage of steel,
    Or continue to scurry on this hamster's wheel?

"I got the inspiration for this one after a visit from my family. They told me that my kids were about to start preschool and I had a feeling of dread that I think any incarcerated parent must feel when this time comes. I shared my feelings with a few other inmates with kids and it helped me a great deal to cope. This essay, another one I entered into a writing competition, also won first place."

• • • •

The best part of my day is whenever my children come to visit me. All the shadows and darkness in my life are banished under the brightness of their presence. They smile and laugh with such sweet innocence that I often pray that they'll never grow up. Unfortunately, I'm certain that there will come a day when life dispels that innocence. They'll discover that there is no Santa Claus, no Easter Bunny and what it means that Daddy is on Death Row.

There is no easy way to talk to my children about the broken path that has led me here. They wouldn't understand all the complexities involved or, worse, they would understand all too well. I don't want it to be me and my situation that drains the wonder from their eyes and replaces it with cynicism. I need them to believe as much as I do that there will be a reprieve for me, that I will find a way home to them.

In a perfect world, children grow up to be untainted by the sins of their parents, but I know that reality is far different. Growing up will be difficult enough without the awkwardness of explaining to their friends about a father who is in prison. I just hope that I won't somehow be the architect of any additional pressures they might be burdened with. I can tell that they possess the strength of character to cope with all that life has to throw at them, but how many scars will they collect before it's all said and done?

During our visits, I do my best to reinforce the delusion that everything, if not normal, is still okay. I laugh, joke and behave as if I have no worries because how I act with them is the one thing I can still truly control. My children, for the most part, pretend along with me, but it feels wrong somehow, almost disingenuous. It leaves a knot in my stomach because, at any time, the slightest of nudges can send my house of cards tumbling down. When the time comes, the nudging needs to be done by me, on my terms, and no one else's.

It's said that everyone is the sum total of all their experiences, whether those experiences be good or bad. I'm curious as to how my situation will factor into the sum total of my children's experiences. Will the positive outweigh the negative? I truly believe that if I knew then what I know now, I would have made different life choices and avoided this broken path that I'm on right now. Yet, a small part of me also wishes for the opposite, which is to know now what I knew then. That way, I could possess a bit of my children's innocence and they wouldn't be the only ones who still believed in Santa Claus and the Easter Bunny.

"This poem came to me after the first phase of my appeal was filed and, subsequently, denied. My then attorney told me not to be discouraged, that there was a long road ahead for me to travel and to stay the course."

. . . .

We twist and turn
    on a marionette's string,
    Never to know
    what the fates will bring.
    Our blood was spent
    on tasks so dark,
    Final leg of our journey
    about to embark.
    The future lost
    to the echo of the past,
    Yet we hold steady,
    vigilant to the last.
    The day approaches
    when our sun may set,
    Our breaths are bated,
    final wagers bet.
    The cliff begins to crumble
    beneath our weight,
    Still we hope, we pray
    it's not too late.
    Our hearts will soar,
    our souls will sing,
    When at last it's cut,
    this marionette's string.

"I'm a huge sports fan and my baseball team is the Chicago Cubs. My eldest sister had moved from Arizona to somewhere close to Kansas City and, one summer, my other sister and I went to visit her. Best vacation EVER!"

. . . .

When people hear the name 'Wrigley Field', they automatically think of America's pastime, baseball, and the Chicago Cubs, but, when I hear it, I think of the vacation I spent with my two sisters one summer in Chicago.

As a lifelong Cubs fan, it had always been a dream of mine to make the pilgrimage to Wrigley Field. I call it a pilgrimage because there is no other word adequate to describe it. Within the sports world, Wrigley Field is an iconic location, a virtual cathedral where the hopes of an entire nation of Cubbie fans are raised, then dashed, where hearts are broken and mended. It's where a single act can lead to an eternal superstition and a World Series title is capable of exorcising a century-long curse of futility. It's baseball history wrapped up in pinstripes, bricks and ivy and put on display in front of rooftop bleachers.

As I walked through those hallowed gates, I forever became part of something greater, more humbling than I could ever imagined. I bought a program, browsed the memorabilia shops and gaped at all the historical displays before stepping out onto the grandstand.

The first thing I noticed was how vibrant everything looked. The brown dirt of the infield, the green outfield grass, the white chalk lines, everything seemed so much sharper to my eyes that afternoon. The next thing I noticed was the smell. Decades of spilt beer, dropped hot dogs, nachos and popcorn trampled into the cement by stomping, cheering feet had soaked into the very foundation of the stands to create a malodorous stench that permeated the air, made even more pungent by the heat and humidity. During the 'seventh inning stretch', a minor celebrity butchered "Take Me Out To The Ballgame', but the crowd didn't care, and neither did I, as we sang jubilantly along. I wanted to weep for the joy of it all.

I don't recall the game itself save that the Cubs won. Their opponent was unimportant as the contest felt almost secondary, that only the experience of attending a game at Wrigley Field was what was significant. It transcended such mundane details as the score, the opposition or the Cubs' division standing. I was in Chicago, at Wrigley Field, watching a Cubs game and nothing else mattered. It was the memory of a lifetime.

Sitting on Death Row is a lonely endeavour. Late at night, when the lights are out, we are often plagued by insomnia as anxiety and bleak thoughts swirl in our minds. When that happens to me, I close my eyes and recall that day. I remember the sights, the sounds and, yes, even the stench, and I smile. Whatever the world may take from me, whether it be my freedom or my life, they can never take that from me. They can never take my Wrigley Memories.

"Everyone has a story and no two are alike. This essay was about another inmate's story and is another one of my favourites. It also won first place, but I was prouder of how moved Cookie was that I would share a part of his story when it was so close to ending. It reminded me that even the simplest of gestures can have the greatest impact in another's life."

. . . .

Life is made up of moments. Short moments, long moments and life changing moments, each leading into the next until your life becomes one continuous string of moments. Sometimes, moments pass by without us even knowing it, while others are all too obvious.

I remember a moment that has just recently transpired. It was a moment I shared with a fellow inmate here on Death Row. This inmate is on the short list for execution, pending only his death warrant being issued. We call him Cookie and he's a Native American from a local reservation.

We were outside for our recreation time, which is nothing more than switching an indoor cage with an outdoor one, but at least we get fresh air and a view of the sky. The cages are situated side by side and when we were brought out, Cookie and I had two cages that were adjacent to each other. It was early evening and cool for Arizona weather. The sun was close to setting behind two mountains in the distance, turning the sky into a kaleidoscope of brilliant colours.

After admiring the scenery for a moment, Cookie pointed just to the north of where the sun was setting. 'My mother's house is just past that mountain,' he said. Then, with a wistful quality to his voice, he added, 'This will probably be the last sunset I ever see.'

There are times, moments, when the best thing to do is say nothing because nothing needs to be said. This, perhaps, was one of those moments, but as I looked at my friend, recognized the tenor and depth of his statement, I found myself saying, 'Right now, at this moment, you and your mother are watching the same sunset.'

Cookie spared me a brief look before turning back to the sight of the setting sun. There had been a wealth of meaning in that look, unspoken words and emotions that only an inmate on Death Row can know and understand. It was a moment of silence for the things we had lost, the things we had gained and the possibilities never to come.

Once the moment had passed, there were probably a dozen things that Cookie could have said, but all he did was give me a short, decisive nod before saying, 'Yeah.'

I couldn't have said it better myself.

"This was the hardest essay for me to write and then share by entering it into another writing competition. My aunt's passing and the inmate's execution had such a profound impact on me that it changed my perspective on my own personal struggles of being on Death Row. It won second place that year, but only because, I think, 'A Moment in Time' won first."

• • • •

As a kid growing up, I'd spend a lot of my summer days hanging around a pond behind my house. It wasn't that large a pond, but it quickly became my one place where I could relax by myself undisturbed.

This pond had a smooth mirror-like quality that could reflect the sky in its surface, and I'd spend hours gazing at the water, enjoying the serenity it offered. Every so often, though, I'd toss a pebble into the centre of the pond, creating wave-like ripples that would radiate outwards in ever-expanding rings until they would reach the edge of the pond.

It would always fascinate me that a mere pebble could incite such a dynamic reaction. After a moment, the ripples would dissipate, and the pond would return to its tranquil stillness. Now, looking back on my time at that pond with those ripples my pebbles would create, two people come to mind.

The first is my aunt, who only just recently passed away. The second is an inmate I've recently met here on death row. They've both led extremely different lives, each making their own unique splashes and ripples which have affected me, as well as others, in a multitude of ways.

My aunt was a remarkable woman, making her ripples as a wife, a mother and a schoolteacher. Married to my uncle for over fifty years, she helped raise two children while teaching many others in her classroom. She taught in the United States and also abroad in countries such as

Kuwait, Brazil and Indonesia, just to name a few. Overall, her travels have taken her to over forty different countries. My aunt, as she battled cancer, became a source of inspiration, courage and resilience that transcended the illness that would ultimately claim her. Her passing wasn't just a loss for my uncle or my family, but for the world as well.

As for the inmate, now that his 'date' has been set, it's a certainty that the controversy constantly surrounding the death penalty will ensure that the ripples of his splash will stretch out to all of death row. Yet, despite this sobering turn of events, he maintains a cheerful dignity that is both admirable and humbling. Just knowing that we may potentially share the same fate has made meeting him and observing the manner in which he carries himself an unforgettable and rewarding experience.

Being on death row, I wonder about a great many things. I wonder what type of splash and ripples I've created in my life and whom they have touched. I wonder whether my own passing will be remarked upon or if I will simply be forgotten. I wonder what splash and ripple my children will make in their own lives. In the end, all I really hope for, at least for my children's lives anyway, is the bigger the splash, the better.

# Two Hours of Madness

"This poem came right after Joseph Woods' execution. All of us on Death Row followed this debacle on TV as best we could. It was a fiasco, start to finish, and generated such an angry reaction from everyone that I felt I needed to express myself with something, anything. This is what came out."

. . . .

Strapped to a table,
    Put on display.
    Watched by voyeurs,
    Actors in a play.
    Their eyes are shrouded,
    Full of hate,
    Eager for blood,
    Harbingers of fate.
    His skin is pierced,
    With needles so cold.
    His eyes drift shut,
    This story foretold.
    Yet the tale spins on,
    Two hours or more.
    Gasping for air,
    Death a distant shore.
    With one final breath,
    Expiring at last,
    His spirit is free,
    His torment past.

"Mental health is a hot button issue nowadays. This is even more true for people incarcerated. This short story was inspired by another inmate here that struggles with it constantly. I seriously question if he shouldn't be housed in a mental ward instead of with us. I don't know how his mind and thoughts work, but I can only guess, based on what I've seen and heard of him. This is how I imagine it."

• • • •

The fluorescent lights in the cell flicker on and he blinks at the sudden brightness.

It has been almost 72 hours since he last slept, since the last time the voices were silent, since the last time he had peace.

The voices are always there, waiting, lurking, biding their time. Sometimes, they are loud, screaming, cursing at him. Sometimes, they are quiet, insidious, manipulative.

It is these second voices he fears the most because they tell him to do things, say things. Things he wished he could forget, things he can't take back.

He's learned to ignore the quiet voices, but, sometimes, they crawl under his skin, invading his flesh, flow through his blood.

The voices are clever, too. They hide in the walls, his mattress, the toilet, the water, even the very air. Sometimes, they mimic other peoples' voices so they can slip inside his mind when he least expects it. Sometimes, they hide in his clothes, making him tear them off his body. Sometimes, the only way to be free of them is to scream so loud that he can't hear anything else. Sometimes, it works. Sometimes, it doesn't... sometimes... sometimes...

He is tired, so very tired, but he dares not sleep. He can hear them now, murmuring in the floor, waiting for him. He covers his head with his blanket, but the voices pass through it like a sieve, singing to him, crooning, mocking, beckoning.

'Little pig, little pig, let me in...' over and over again, they whisper.

Hysterical laughter boils out of him, and he screams back, 'Not by the hair of my chinny, chin-chin!'

The voices increase in volume. 'I'll huff, I'll puff, I'll blow your door in!'

He covers his ears with his hands, clutching at his hair, yelling obscenities, vainly trying to drown the voices out.

'LITTLE PIG, LITTLE PIG, LET ME IN!'

'Ahhhhhhhh!'

The voices are under his feet, digging beneath his toenails. He jumps up, slapping at his toes, but it's too late. The voices are in him now, worming their way into his veins, his bones, his muscle and sinew.

They are in his ankles, spreading up to his calves, his thighs. He is frantic, clawing at his skin, bleeding where his nails find purchase.

'Noooooooo!'

They are in his stomach, his chest, his throat, reverberating with their commands, their instructions.

'LET ME IN! LET ME IN!'

They are in his mouth, his nose, behind his eyes. He is suffocating, terrified of giving in, but unable to resist.

He bangs his head against the wall again and again, screaming.

'NOT BY THE HAIR OF MY CHINNY, CHIN-CHIN!'

Suddenly, the voices are gone. They disappear like a wisp of smoke in a summer breeze.

He is on his knees, quietly weeping, his tears mingling with the blood from his split scalp. He is drained, exhausted, spent. Darkness creeps into his vision and, as he collapses in the blessed silence, he wonders how long before the voices will come again...

"If you've ever heard the phrase 'prison changed you', it's probably a true statement. I'm so different from the man I was before coming to prison that it sometimes boggles my mind. I wanted to express that feeling in some way, which resulted in this story. It only won second place that year but is one of more most personal works."

· · · ·

What would it be like to be free? Free of this prison cell, free of punishment, free to live my life with my family. Would I forget my time of incarceration, all the indignities and humiliations heaped upon me? Or would I carry it with me on the Outside like a yoke around my neck, dragging me down so that my liberation is nothing more than an illusion?

Would the friends that abandoned me flock back to my side or would they turn the other way if they saw me on the street? Would they even remember me? Would I even remember what it was like to be myself before I became 'him', the convict, the felon, the criminal? Have I lost that last bit of innocence that we all carry, or will it return with time?

I see myself as I am right now, hard and cynical. I see myself as I was, cheerful and oblivious in my naiveté. What will I see when I look in the mirror if I am freed? What about a decade from now if I'm not? Will I become one of the faceless convicts that rotate in and out, angry and bitter, always on the cusp of violence? Or will I retain a shred of my identity to nurture the flame of hope that burns in my heart?

I doubt anyone I knew could recall me as I was if they were to see me now. In turn, I would see them as they were and not who they have become. Familiar faces on complete strangers.

Every day I exist here, I encounter the same things. There is a comfort to the routine, a rhythm to the monotony that acts as a buffer to the negativity that only despair can inspire. There are the faceless 'badges' that represent all the injustices of the prison system. There are the nameless prisoners that stand in defiance, refusing to acknowledge their defeat. Do any of us see each other as real men, as individuals, or have we become nothing more than familiar strangers with different faces?

I imagine how I would do it all over again, the choices I would make, the paths I would journey upon. I've experienced and seen so much waste, so much loss, and, yet time marches on, waiting for no one. Despite how much I've changed, I'm still caught in a state of arrested development. There is no growth where I am at, only stagnation. Meanwhile, on the Outside, in the real world, my children are maturing, my parents continue to get older, and life just happens.

For me, one thing remains certain. If I want things to change, it will be up to me and no one else. If I don't, I'm afraid that one day I'll wake up, look in the mirror and be faced with just another familiar stranger.

# A Tale of Frank & Frank's Revenge

"Insects. Bugs. Pests. Doesn't matter what kind as I've learned to hate them all. When I was housed at Central Unit, the building I was in was condemned. Seriously. DOC had to pay an annual fine for keeping human beings in that building. The construction was shoddy, as was the plumbing, which led to all manners of infestations from flies and mosquitoes, to spiders and the focus of these two tales, cockroaches. I have my moments of levity that I often express in my writing, and I have embellished things for comedic effect, but this is based on ACTUAL events. Really."

· · · ·

**A Tale of Frank**

One day coming out of my cell, I encountered a roach unlike any that I had ever seen: the length of a playing card and about an inch and a half wide, the colour of burnt chocolate and antennae that moved with preternatural intelligence. I immediately named him 'Frank' after Danny DeVito's character on 'It's Always Sunny in Philadelphia' and swore I would bring about Frank's destruction. Much to my dismay, Frank had other plans.

I raised my foot high, intending to crush him beneath my heel. Yet, in the fraction of a second it took to bring my foot down, Frank .... moved. One moment, he was where my foot would have slammed down, the next, Frank was almost 10 feet away! I gasped in shock at Frank's speed and elusiveness. Yet, the most impressive aspect of his escape from doom was that Frank had moved so swiftly and was still able to be facing me, antennae twitching, mocking me .... I took an involuntary step back and Frank moved with me, shadowing my step so that the distance between us remained the same. I knew for certain then that Frank was no ordinary roach, but something worse, something malevolent, perhaps vegan ....

I found my courage again and made to finish Frank off once and for all. I knew by doing so, the world would be a safer, less creepy place. Plus, Frank gave me the heebie-jeebies. However, as I sallied forth, Frank sped away into the stairwell and beyond my reach. I was certain Frank, and I would meet again.

It was several days before I would catch a glimpse of my arch nemesis. It was in the stairwell that I saw him, surrounded by a bevy of his subordinates, roaches of intermediate sizes, many tiny, others larger, but none as impressive as Frank. Frank must have sensed my presence because he turned, antennae twitching, to face me. Then, he was gone, his followers scattering in all directions.

That night, I discovered a roach in my cell, nosing about my garbage can. It wasn't hard to squish him, but, still, it left me with a sense of foreboding. For the next week, I would find one, maybe two roaches in or around my cell, probing and testing my defences every day. No other inmate saw more than one the entire week. It was then that I was certain that Frank was coming for me ....

I continue to see Frank scuttling about, watching me from the shadows, waiting for the right moment to strike. I sometimes forget about him as I go about my day. Then, I will turn around and he is there for a moment, then gone, waiting only long enough to make certain that I had seen him. Frank haunts my dreams, keeping me up at night ... I will crush him one day, but that day hasn't come. Until then, the war continues ...

• • • •

**Frank's Revenge**

So, there I was... it was midday and I'd just finished working out and needed to shower.

I collected my shower gear and proceeded to the shower stall located in the front half of the pod. There are only two shower stalls on my run, and I prefer the one in the front because it's more private than the one in the back.

My muscles were sore, so I decided to let the hot water beat on my body before actually washing. After a minute or two of blissful water therapy, I shampooed my hair and began to soap up with my Old Spice body wash (shameless product plug). However, when I turned to rinse off my chiselled, manly chest (humble brag) of the soapy suds, I let out a squeak that wasn't at all girlish or anything. I swear. It was more of a macho bellow. In a slightly higher than normal register... accompanied by a teeny, tiny little hop. I may have soiled myself... but probably not. Probably.

On the shower wall, at eye level, just under the shower head where I was about to duck my head under was a ginormous, terrifyingly monstrous cockroach! It wasn't Frank sized... but damn close. And it was looking at me... judging me even. It was also, I swear to you, crouched like it was getting ready to leap at me like a Japanese Kamikaze, ready to commit suicide if only it could take me with it.

A daunting sight to be sure... I won't say that I fled the shower half-washed with only a towel to preserve my modesty, but I departed with haste before this interloper could attack me. I came back armed with a hefty broom to smite this wicked creature, but when I looked... it was gone. I finished my shower, watchful and wary... and in the shower stall in the back half of the pod.

"This short essay was based on the evolving relationship that I have with my kids. They continue to shock, please and leave me in bewilderment as they've grown up. I love them and am so very proud of them. This received an Honourable Mention from a competition I entered in the non-fiction category from my alma mater, The University of Arizona."

• • • •

Being a father is hard. Just ask any father, they'll back me up.

Being a father of twin girls is even harder.

Now imagine those twins' becoming teenagers, just getting their driver's licenses and being sexually active.

Getting nervous? Wait, there's more!

How about being a father where one of the twins now identifies as male and the other twin is dating both girls and boys? Just trying to unpack that whole situation is enough to cause premature hair loss.

Throw in being a father who has been in prison since the twins were less than two years old and you can imagine how I might be struggling to present myself as an authoritative presence in their lives.

For instance, try giving fatherly advice to your twins when they're teenagers in high school... well, you might have more success convincing a Trump supporter that the election wasn't rigged.

If things weren't bad enough, then there's the pandemic. Fear of the coronavirus spreading through the prison caused them to shut down visitations for well over a year, so your beautifully complicated children are going through the most confusing and wonderful times of their lives and there's no way for you to guide them or even just be there for them. It's a level of frustration that's almost unbearable. Then, when they do resume visits, they are non-contact, so even when they are there, you can't even give them a hug.

Then, you have a surreal moment that seems to epitomize the whole situation...

At the second visit since visitation has resumed, your kids are comparing knee scrapes. One, who works as a carhop at a local fast-food restaurant, fell during work and the other, a bit of a clumsy kid, just plain tripped. Well, they pull up their pant legs and show their respective injuries. Much to your surprise, the twin who now identifies as male has more hair on their leg than you.

You make a joke about it to cover up your shock, but your child replies quite seriously, 'I'll die before I shave again.'

Sometimes, there are situations that demand action, others inaction, but in this situation, all you can do is surrender and wave the white flag. Your darling twins aren't the adoring kids who you could bounce on your knee. Instead, they are young adults who have developed into sophisticated human beings with a definitive view of the world and their place in it. Their guidelines are provided by social media and reality TV stars.

So, what's a father to do?

You go with it.

You support and love them unconditionally. You learn about TikTok, YouTube and keep up with the Kardashian's. You listen and learn that while you've been in prison, the world has been going at light speed. Your children have cell phones that are more powerful than the fastest computer that you've ever seen or used. Your kids are better informed of world events than you are and have opinions on everything... and aren't shy about sharing them. You learn new terminology like what it means to be 'woke' or 'pansexual' and why veganism isn't the insidious trend you thought it would be. You listen and you learn.

Being a father is hard, but rewarding in ways you could never have imagined. All you have to do is remember that even though you are in prison, you are still able to be a part of their lives. You become what they need you to be: a Millennial Dad.

"This was the other story I entered in the same competition as 'Millennial Dad', but in the fiction category, where it also received an Honourable Mention. The story was inspired by another inmate who had befriended what we call a 'yard cat'. All the details are fictionalized or embellished save for the name the inmate had given his cat: Quencher."

• • • •

When the inmate woke up, he waited impatiently for the guards to open his cell door, almost bouncing on his toes in eagerness. In his hand, he held an unopened package of tuna that he had purchased from canteen along with a plastic spork. Quencher would be hungry and probably yowling for the inmate.

Quencher was an especially mangy cat, half his tail gone, ending in a scarred stump, fur matted and missing in clumps. But this wasn't unusual for a cat of Quencher's status. You see, Quencher was a prison yard cat. That meant that Quencher had to literally scratch and claw for survival, for every scrap of food or water.

The inmate also led a difficult life. Born into poverty in an economically depressed part of the city, the inmate never had the opportunity for any life beyond that of gang violence, drugs and general criminality. He quit school in his early teens and had a juvenile record to make any social worker cringe before turning 18. From there, he was in and out of prison for the next several years before bottoming out and, in a drug-fuelled rage, earning the life sentence he was currently serving. He was now entering the prison system a damaged and broken man, lost without any chance of salvation, angry and resentful at life.

The first ten years of the inmate's sentence was served with multiple disciplinary violations, assaults and rampant drug use. The inmate was well on his way to an early prison grave in Potter's field when something wondrous happened. That something was the appearance of a mangy cat.

The inmate was just back from a two-week stint in the 'hole' after getting high and assaulting another inmate. He was dope sick and, truthfully, feeling sorry for himself. He'd always tried to numb his rage and pain with life through drugs or violence, but after this last trip to the hole, it just wasn't enough. The inmate was exhausted, both in his heart and his soul. In the chow hall that day, he sat with his lunch tray, uneaten because he wasn't able to keep anything down, and contemplated what was left for him. He had no family willing to write or even accept his calls, much less visit, and he'd never been one for religion. In short, he felt all alone.

Then, the inmate heard a sound he hadn't heard on the yard before. It was the yowl of a cat. But it wasn't the sound of any kind of cat that the inmate had heard before. This sound was pitiful and full of despair. It was a sound that seemed to resonate with the way the inmate was feeling. So, when the inmate turned around and saw this mangy cat poking around the dumpster as if looking for a way to get inside, instead of ignoring it, the inmate opened his tray, took out whatever mystery meat that they were serving in the chow hall and tossed it over to where the cat was. And so, it began.

From that day on, the inmate began to seek out that mangy cat with only half a tail. He'd leave out food for him if he couldn't find him, but when he did find him, he wouldn't leave until he was sure the cat had eaten. As for his peers, they silently wondered if the inmate had finally snapped, especially when he named the cat Quencher.

It took almost a month before the cat finally allowed the inmate to even pet him, but, in that time, something had changed for them both. They had both begun to heal. For Quencher, there wasn't the same struggle to survive that it had been forced to endure. It had a steady source of nourishment now and a unique feeling of safety whenever the inmate was nearby. For the inmate, there was a sense of satisfaction in caring for something for no other reason than he could. So, when he noticed that the mangy cat, despite its many scars, wasn't so mangy anymore, had begun to gain weight and overall, just seemed healthier, something broken inside the inmate began to mend. His mood was better and his anger, while still there, was somehow muted. It was an incredible transformation for both cat and inmate.

So, now, when the inmate wakes up, he has a purpose, a goal. It isn't just to feed a mangy, prison yard cat, though, it's what the inmate needs to keep going... to survive.

"Prison nicknames. I have one, as do a great many other inmates. You get one a wide variety of ways. Some come to prison with one, others earn theirs inside, while others just fall into them for the most random reasons. The thing with prison nicknames is that they are given to you by others, you never get to pick your own. Mine, 'Vegas', was given to me because I used to deal poker in Las Vegas, no other reason. This story is about how a twenty plus year convict finally earned his nickname. It also evokes the phrase: 'You can't make this shit up!' - no pun intended."

• • • •

I have to tell you a story that YOU in particular will find horrific about an acquaintance of mine named Joe. Well, we were at rec and Joe had a gastric 'emergency'.

I want to preface this by saying that I HAD toilet paper, as did several other inmates, but Joe did NOT ask for it from anybody because, if he had, we certainly would have given him some.

At the start of this episode, I was sitting under the veranda on the other side of the yard playing pinochle. Someone said, 'Look over there at Joe!'. Well, I looked, and Joe was sitting on the toilet taking a shit. (Our bathrooms are open air for security reasons, so we saw everything.) THEN, he took the bandana off his HEAD and proceeded to wipe his ass with it. (Yuk!)

I want to intercede at this point to say that if I had been in that position and had to resort to my bandana, I'm tossing that bandana into the garbage, period, end of story. Well, not Joe.

What Joe did was take that bandana, with his shit on it, and rinsed it out in the drinking fountain that we all use to get water or wash our hands. I was stunned, disgusted and, somehow, vastly amused even as I felt a bit sorry for him. Then, to top it all off, he brought his shitty bandana, even rinsed out, to the veranda where we were all sitting and draped it over a table on the other side from where I was so he could dry it out. (Double Yuk!!)

Vinnie, a loud Italian inmate, was there and just gave him the business until Joe went to a CO and went in, claiming that he wasn't feeling well. As expected, Joe didn't come out the next day to either rec or chow, though he did the day after.

Then, when he ran into Jimmy, a guy I call Other Asian, Jimmy said, 'What's up, Doo Doo Joe?'. (Pause to laugh) Joe flipped him off and now everyone calls him Doo Doo Joe.

Anyway, Joe has since been resentenced, rolled up and moved into the building next door. But there is a saying or universal truth, if you like, that goes: 'There are NO secrets in the penitentiary.' The tale of Doo Doo Joe has already spread through his new building and, well, I've heard he's been having a rough go of it. Either way, the next time he goes to rec, I hope he remembers to pack a spare role of toilet paper. Just in case.

"I've been told that I have a very self-deprecating manner sometimes and that I don't take things or myself seriously enough. In part, this is true, but I also think that I enjoy a bit of silliness and levity, especially in a place like Death Row. I always try and find that silver lining in dark clouds or just something that will make me, or others smile or laugh. That being said, I wrote this to amuse my wife, friends and family about some of the more mundane things that I do here that they might not know (or WANT to know). This happened. Really."

• • • •

Its hot out, the sun shining bright in the Arizona sky. Its rec time and the yard is full of inmates scattered about. They're dressed in shorts and t-shirts with a few who have shed their tops in response to the temperature, letting the sun beat down on their bare skin.

Vegas is one of those inmates who is enjoying rec. He needs the fresh air and open sky to counter the dreariness of confinement. Once rec is done, he'll get a shower, but, after that, its lockdown for the rest of the day. So, he enjoys what little freedom comes his way.

Normally, Vegas would be playing basketball, working out or playing cards with his friends, but not today. Today is a special day, one that comes about once every six weeks. Nobody else has a day like this. It's a special day, one reserved only for Vegas. It's not a holiday, so it's not something he necessarily celebrates more than suffers through. But in many ways, it is necessary.

Vegas has a problem. He would say it's an 'issue', but his friends are very adamant that it IS a 'problem'. His wife, when she hears about his 'issue', usually just shakes her head, puts her fingers in her ears and goes, 'La-la-la-la-la!'. But nobody is perfect.

Vegas has body hair. And not just body hair, but BODY HAIR. He has hair on his face, his legs, his chest, even small coarse hairs that sprout from the curve of his inner ear. And he has back hair. Long curly black hair that covers his back and shoulders much like the pelt of a bear. It's not the usual amount of hair that one finds on someone of Asian descent. However, he is only half Asian on his mother's side. The truly bizarre thing is that even his father, whom you would think to be the genetic culprit of his hair dilemma, doesn't have the hair issues that his son does.

So, the day that comes about every six weeks is Shearing Day.

Shearing Day is comparable to the spring shearing of sheep, but Vegas is no sheep. He is a man... with friends. Unrelentingly sarcastic and judgemental friends with long memories and scathing opinions that they aren't shy about sharing. Vegas knows all this, but Shearing Day is a necessity. His hair grows so quickly and so thickly that he cannot allow it to go on for too long. A hairy Vegas is a cranky Vegas.

The complication is that Vegas is also a larger than average man with muscular arms. His arms are so muscular that he is unable to reach around his body to shave his back on his own. So, he must enlist help. Enter Paul.

Paul and Vegas have been friends for years. Their relationship is such that Vegas feels comfortable asking for Paul's assistance in this endeavour without fear of judgement or recrimination. Paul's personality is, for lack of a better term, quirky, so he's more than willing to help with this.

Vegas tracks Paul down and motions him over to the barber area where inmates are allowed to get their hair cut using clippers that the administration provides.

When Paul approaches, Vegas simply says, 'It's time.'

Paul solemnly nods, saying nothing. He knows what day it is and what his task is.

Walking over to the barber box where several clippers are stored, Paul spares a glance at Vegas's back to see its condition. Nodding solemnly again, Paul selects the pair of clippers with widest blade head and strongest motor. It's a pair of industrial clippers, because Paul knows that it's the only pair strong enough to handle this job.

Vegas seats himself on one of the metal stools used by inmates getting haircuts. Once he's settled in, he utters those fateful words:

'Shear me, Paul!'

So, it begins...

There's a click and hum when Paul activates the clippers. Its louder than the other clippers to coincide with its size and capabilities. Even the clippers seem to understand the daunting breadth of the assignment.

Paul passes the clippers over Vegas's back. His hands are steady and sure. This isn't his first rodeo. He shaves quickly back and forth, then up and down. It's a weighty task and takes time. Soon, there are small tufts of hair dropping to the ground at Paul's feet, not dissimilar to a blizzard... but with dark coarse back hair shaped like tiny little balls.

Ten minutes later, Paul needs a break. The heat of the Arizona sun and his labours are making him sweat so much that the clippers have grown slippery in his hands. He wipes his hands dry of sweat and guzzles water from a bottle before resuming.

Once it's done, Paul uses a small horsehair brush often seen in barbershops to brush away any stray hairs so he can make sure of the completion of the job. Satisfied, he puts away the clippers while Vegas stands to brush off his shorts of stray hairs.

Vegas turns to Paul. No words are spoken. Vegas nods to Paul. Paul nods back. Then, as one, they turn and walk away in opposite directions.

Another Shearing Day is done, and Vegas feels as if a weight has, quite literally, been lifted off his back. He revels in his hairless condition because he knows it won't last. He knows that in about six weeks, he'll be saying those words again:

'Shear me, Paul!'

# Untitled Haiku & Lord of the Crickets

"These are two short poems I wrote over a decade apart. The first, the haiku, was written right after I was sentenced and came to Death Row. It was snapshot into my thoughts, the anxiety and uncertainty that I initially felt. The second, of course, is a take on the inscription on the Ring of Power from Lord of the Rings incorporated with my love of fantasy, hatred of the insects that would sneak into my cell and the more light-hearted mentality I've adopted since meeting my darling wife, Vicki. I think the contrast says much about the growth and evolution of my mental health since I've come here."

• • • •

**Untitled Haiku**
> Petals in the wind
> Swirl recklessly in my mind
> Never to take flight.

• • • •

**Lord of the Crickets**
> One cricket to sneak inside,
> One cricket to hop,
> One shoe to smoosh them all,
> And, with a hard whack... POP!

# The Pandemic – A Collection of Three Stories

**- The Great Corona Virus Swab**

**- Off to see the Wizard, the Wonderful Wizard of Vaccines**

**- Curse of the Stygian Witches**

"The pandemic lockdown was hard on everyone. It created a lot of unexpected difficulties in everyone's lives. For those of us in prison, it created even more separation from our loved ones and a return to isolation as we were locked down the entire time. When they finally tested us and administered the vaccine, I chose to write these three anecdotes to help diminish the dread and fear we felt if we ever, in fact, contracted the Corona virus. These were sent out as email blasts, so the tenor is a bit different from my other stories. Plus, ignore my references to organ harvesting as I have an irrational fear that DOC will do just that as a way to generate more income to meet their budget. I don't actually think they will. Kinda. Also, our nurses are really lovely people and not blood hungry witches. Probably."

• • • •

**The Great Corona Virus Swab**

It is done.

Central Unit has been completely tested for the coronavirus. It was a harrowing experience and here is how it went...

First, they've put the whole unit on lockdown, presumably, until the test results come back, so that sucks, but it is what it is. Anyway, they marched us out of our building, masks on, and told us to go to the chow hall the long way around. That means we had to enter a certain door to be processed. By the way, anyone who refused testing was to be immediately sent to Kasson Unit, AKA the medical unit, for automatic quarantine.

Well, when we entered, I saw that the whole chow hall was filled with medical personnel ready to test us. A guard checked us in, one by one, and we each spoke with a 'screener' to go over some paperwork and answer some basic questions like: What race are you? What ethnicity are you? (Those were back-to-back questions) Are you symptomatic? (duh) Are you pregnant? (really) etc., so forth and so on.

Then, once the questions were done, we were sent to the next phase where we were to have our brains 'tickled' with a swab. Not a very appealing occurrence, so I did my best to search out a tester with 'kind' eyes since they were all wearing masks, of course. Side note, they all were wearing these grey lab coats like evil scientists or a Bond villain ready to release a biological weapon to conquer the world... or maybe I was just projecting.

Here's how the testing went...

Tester: Hi, how are you?

Me: I'm fine, how are you?

Tester: Good. Now I'm going to stick about an inch of this swab up one nostril, swirl it around for 5 seconds, then do the other nostril, OK?

Me: Peachy.

Tester: It will feel weird, but you can take it.

Me: (no response)

I tilted my head back; he did the swab and all I wanted to do in that moment as the swab swirled around was sneeze. I held it in because I had this image in my mind, that if I DID sneeze, all the testers would suddenly tackle me for being 'symptomatic', lying on my questionnaire and dragging me off to quarantine. Then, there would be a struggle and I'd shout, 'You can't do this, I'm pregnant!'... Sorry, I have my moments of dramatic silliness and then I move on. After that, we returned to our cells, were locked down and shall remain so for the time being.

• • • •

**Off to see the Wizard, the Wonderful Wizard of Vaccines**

So, there I was, minding my own business, taking a midmorning nap (because that's what I do) when the CO's came and offered myself and three others the opportunity to get our COVID vaccine shot. Of course, once I wiped the boogers from my eyes, I readily agreed.

We departed for the chow hall shortly thereafter and was surprised that the evil scientists were not present. Instead, it was a pair of nurses vaccinating us all. Curiouser and curiouser...

When it was my turn, I signed a shady document that I didn't read because I forgot my glasses, so I probably signed away a kidney or my spleen. They also didn't ask if I was pregnant, so I think we were making progress...

I rolled up my sleeve for the nurse so she could inject me with the vaccine, allowing my arm to dangle loosely by my side. She raised the syringe but didn't inject me. Instead, she frowned and said, 'If you stop flexing, it won't hurt when I inject you.'

I turned my head toward her and said, a little smirk on my lips, 'I'm NOT flexing.'

Her eyes widened a bit and she blushed, clearly embarrassed at her assumption, perhaps a tad impressed with my manliness (humble brag) ... then she jabbed me super hard with the needle, almost making me squeak.

Then, they made us all wait around for 15 minutes to make sure that we didn't experience any immediate side effects. Of course, all they did was ask, 'Is anyone experiencing any shortness of breath?'

We all replied in the negative and, after that exhaustive examination, they sent us on our way.

So endeth my tale of vaccines and flexing.

• • • •

**Curse of the Stygian Witches**

The day started innocently enough... chow, work out, shower and then chow again. It didn't become weird until right before count time...

Someone yelled out, 'Nurses are here for 1, 7, 9 and 10!'

I came out of my cell in surprise because I wasn't expecting nurses to come here as they usually make us go to Medical for our issues or the chow hall for our vaccine shot as they did previously.

There were three of them waiting at the gate, along with a guard. The nurses were all women, masked so that their beady little eyes were all I could see of their faces. They crouched over a pull case, whispering or plotting, if you prefer. I edged my way to the door, which was essentially just another set of bars, with the nurses on the other side from me.

Were they seriously going to inject me through the bars? They didn't pop open the door, so apparently so. The other three inmates went before me as I eyed these three nurses with no small degree of apprehension. They injected my pod mates quickly and sent them on their way, but I swear their eyes lit up when they saw me approach for my shot.

One of them handed me a clipboard. 'Here, sign this.'

I frowned. 'What am I signing?'

'Oh, nothing important,' she said cagily. 'Just something for our records.'

'Do I get a copy?' I inquired.

'No.'

I wasn't sure if I was signing away my organs if I died from the shot or giving up my first-born child, but I scribbled my name down and she snatched the clipboard and scuttled away before I could ask for more details.

The second nurse came up to the bars and said, 'Time for your shot.' I think the two other nurses were rubbing their hands in anticipation or I could have imagined it.

I stepped up (doing my best not to look like I was flexing) and turned so she could reach my arm through the bars. I felt a tiny little prick of pain and heard the nurse say something that chilled me to the bones.

'We have a bleeder!'

What the...?

I looked down at my arm and, sure enough, there was a tiny trickle of blood coming from the injection site. It wasn't that big of a trickle, so I wasn't too concerned, but the nurses' reactions were the polar opposite of mine.

They fairly bounced on their toes with glee as I bled in front of them. Then they turned as one to the pull case, crouching over it, their heads huddled together as the poked around in the depths of the pull case. They whispered to each other in hushed tones, glancing over their shoulders every once in a while, as if to make sure that I wasn't leaving. They looked for all the world like a trio of Stygian witches discussing how best to utilize the blood that I had spilt in their next evil ceremony.

I started to edge away...

'Stop!' the third nurse shouted, and I froze, suddenly comforted by the fact that they were on the other side of the bars.

'Here,' she said, flourishing something at me. That something turned out to be a single unwrapped band aid. 'Let me put this on you.'

I stared at the band aid mistrustfully. 'No, I'm good,' I demurred. 'Thank you though.'

The nurse scowled at me, and, behind her, the other two nurses were watching with an intensity I thought was disproportionate to the situation.

The nurse didn't speak, just held out the band aid expectantly. After a long moment, I plucked it out of her hand with two fingers and made my escape, scurrying back to my cell. Before ducking inside, I risked one final glance at those Stygian nurses and saw that they were still watching me. I wasn't certain, but I think they were chanting something at me through their masks...

I don't know if it was simply side effects from the shot, they gave me or an evil hex that they had cast on me, but I was laid up in my bed with chills and aches all the next day...

So ends my tale of my second vaccine shot...

# A Chilling Tale of Solitude

"I love Halloween. I love the horror movie marathons they show on TV. I love the costumes. I love the idea of walking around and taking candy indiscriminately from strangers. It appeals to my imaginative nature and sense of the supernatural. I also incorporated a bit of the mental health struggles I know that some inmates may go through. Either way, this story gave both my cellie and I the wiggins."

• • • •

The inmate stood in his cell and shivered.

It was winter in Arizona, but winter in Arizona prisons isn't like winter anywhere else in the United States. In Arizona, winter means wearing a sweater, maybe a thermal top, for the inmate. Temperature controlled cells meant that it never got too hot nor too cold, but that wasn't why he shivered.

The building pod where the inmate was housed was a split-level unit with lower and upper tiers situated in a simple horseshoe configuration that help assist with security monitoring. The inmate was housed in a cell on the upper tier on one 'arm' of the horseshoe that faced the other 'arm'. Not every cell had an occupant and there were three cells that were empty, all in a row, opposite of the inmate's cell where he could see them from the window, a long vertical strip of heavy glass, in his door.

All the cells had lights that could be turned on and off by their occupants. The inmate had turned his off so that he stood in darkness, gazing out the window at the three empty cells on the other side of the pod. For whatever reason, despite being empty, the lights were on. The inmate was at the window watching because of something he had seen the previous night. That night, it had been out of the corner of his eye that he'd seen it. A flicker of movement coupled with a feeling of unease. He'd been standing at his cell's sink, brushing his teeth, his routine before retiring for the evening. He'd felt a chill on his skin and turned in confusion. The AC was off, as was his portable fan, so he was unsure what had made his flesh tingle with cold.

When he turned toward the door, something in his peripheral vision grabbed at his attention. It was from one of the empty cells across the way. It was so quick that, except for the sudden ripple of gooseflesh on his arm, he wasn't sure that he had even seen anything at all. He had gone to the window, toothbrush still in his mouth, and peered outside his cell. The pod lights had been turned off, so the lights in the empty cells glared bright in the darkness through the windows of those cells. The inmate had stood there a moment longer before shaking his head and turning back to his task of oral hygiene. As he had shifted, he'd seen something in the first empty cell. It was a shift in the light that had caught his attention. Trepidation had coursed through the inmate. What had he seen? What could it possibly be? Was a guard in there for some reason? If so, why was the door closed?

There had always been talk amongst the inmates that this prison was haunted, but it wasn't anything the inmate had taken seriously. To him, it was the idle talk of men with too much time on their hands. Of course, it didn't help that the guards perpetuated the rumours with talk of their own, but nobody really took them seriously either. And yet... The inmate had stood there, toothbrush still in his mouth, eyes locked on the cell, waiting to see something, anything, to explain what he thought he had seen. After a long minute, he'd finally turned away.

He'd finished brushing, rinsed his mouth out and then washed his face, all the while wondering if he was finally losing it. Prison, especially for those in isolation, could affect men differently. Some became withdrawn, others with mental health problems had had their issues become worse, while others developed mental issues that slowly made them a touch crazy. Was that what was happening to him, he'd wondered. Was he beginning to see things? Was isolation affecting him so severely that his mind had begun playing tricks on him?

The inmate had dried his face and blown out a long breath. He needed to get a grip, he'd decided, just go to bed and forget all about it. He'd nodded to himself and turned to his bunk, ready to go to bed. Yet, he had paused again and, as if of their own volition, his feet had taken him back to his cell door window.

He stood there looking at the window of that first cell long into the night, wondering if he would see it again and terrified that he would. Now, the inmate was standing there again, watching and waiting.

He stood there long into the night... and shivered.

"I've been a lifelong fan of the fantasy genre. Tolkien, Weis and Hickman, Goodkind, Rothfuss, Jordan, Martin, Anthony... the list goes on for authors who have entertained and inspired me. Swords, sorcery, dragons, elves and life under the chivalric code always seemed to capture my imagination and sustained me when I needed an escape from the mundaneness of life. It's been an ambition of mine to write my own story, my own epic saga. With that in mind, here is a short story from the novel I am currently working on, as yet untitled. I deliberately left out the names of the principal characters, though I know who they are, for a reason, choosing instead to go with a more anonymous style I feel is more suited to the method of storytelling. Think of this as a companion story to the larger work, separate, but very much a part of the greater storyline. I hope you like it."

• • • •

It was well past midday when the traveller approached the small town. It wasn't a large town, and the traveller didn't know its name, but it sported a small gatehouse where the road he was on led into it.

As he neared the gatehouse, the traveller saw several men in uniforms milling about. Their uniforms were a light green with gold inlay, the colours of this kingdom's army.

The traveller was dressed lightly in deference to the heat of the day, his cloak rolled up and stored in his pack. Dust from the road he had journeyed upon liberally coated his boots and his shirt clung to his chest with sweat. In one hand, the traveller carried a walking stick that came up to the top of his six-foot frame. A sword was belted at his waist and hung from his left hip, and a long dagger was strapped along his right.

At his appearance, the uninformed men came to attention and spread out across the road, blocking his way. The traveller couldn't say if they were soldiers or simply town guardsman, but by the alert look in their eyes and the stiffness of their postures, he would have guessed the former.

'Hail, traveller,' one called. He was a blocky man, heavy with muscle, a long spear held in one hand, butt ground into the earth. There were four others there of varying size and age and the traveller readjusted his assessment of soldiers to guardsmen. A few may have served in the King's army, but no longer. Two had the steady look of men who had seen battle and survived while the rest had either a bored expression or one that was too eager by half.

'Hail, guardsman,' the traveller said, stopping a respectful distance from the gatehouse that was close enough to be heard clearly without being threatening. Too eager guardsmen, the traveller knew, sometimes swung swords first and asked questions later.

'What business do you have here?' the central guardsman asked.

'I'm seeking a man,' the traveller answered before adding, 'and rest from the road after a long journey.'

'What man?' another guardsman interjected. 'What's his name?'

The one who had spoken was one of the guardsmen with too eager eyes and the traveller could tell that the first guardsman was annoyed that he had spoken at all.

'Are you a bounty hunter?' the too eager guardsman further demanded. 'Because we'll brook no such business in our town.'

'Enough, Layton,' the first guardsman said before turning back to the traveller. 'State your business or be on your way.'

The traveller said, 'I am no bounty hunter, nor do I seek to cause trouble in your fair town. I'm seeking a comrade in arms from the war... and to find respite from my travels, if only for a night.'

'Which war did you serve in?' the guardsman asked. 'You don't look old enough to have fought in many.'

'One war is enough for any man, though I have fought in several,' he replied. 'The one I refer to was Greenshire.'

There were several hisses and the sucking in of breaths at the name before the guardsman asked, 'You were at Greenshire?'

'Aye.'

'I fought at Greenshire,' the guardsman said. 'And a sorry bit of business it was.'

The traveller said nothing but acknowledged his statement with a soldier's salute, fist to heart. The guardsman returned the gesture solemnly before saying, 'Not many survived that war and few enough of them are here. Who is it that you seek?'

'I don't know his name, but would know him nonetheless,' the traveller answered.

'Bollocks!' the Layton spat. 'You seek a man whose name you don't know in a town you never been too? For what reason? Nothing good, I say!'

The traveller turned to Layton and said, 'There were many men, both alive or fallen, whose names I did not know. As for my business with him, I simply want to share a tale and perhaps a drink. Nothing more.' Cutting a look at the central guardsman, he quietly added, 'If you had fought at Greenshire, you would understand.'

Stung, Layton took a step forward, spear lowered. 'Git on with you, stranger! You'll find no succour here!'

'Leave off, Layton,' a voice quietly said from inside the gatehouse.

At those words, Layton immediately snapped to attention and stepped back. He said nothing more, but his eyes were furious, and neck flushed at the perceived slight.

The traveller turned as another guardsman stepped into the open. This one was older, grizzled, but in no way infirm. His hair was cut short and shot through with grey. He had a square, smooth shaven jaw and sported a long scar that bisected one cheek just short of his piercing blue eyes. He had the bearing of a soldier and one used to having his commands obeyed. His frame was slighter than that of the traveller, but he moved with the confidence of a man who could handle himself well against any opponent. A gold epaulet was draped over one shoulder and the guardsmen, as one, all stood straighter at his appearance.

This guardsman strode forward to look the traveller in the eye from a mere arm's length. They locked gazes for a long moment and the traveller felt something pass between them, a decision that the guardsman had come to.

'We boast only a single inn,' the guardsman said. 'But it has a bath and passable food and drink. You have leave to stay a single night but must go come the morrow.'

'But Captain!' Layton, unable to contain himself, complained. 'This stranger...'

Layton's voice trailed off when the guardsman turned and looked at him, saying nothing. His look had been blank, almost lazily so, but it was enough to make Layton's face drain of colour and drop his eyes. 'Apologies, Captain,' he murmured contritely.

When he turned back around, the traveller spoke. 'My thanks, Captain.'

The traveller was answered with nothing but a dip of the guardsman chin.

The guardsmen parted to allow the traveller through and as he made to move past them, the guardsman said quietly, 'My duty ends after eighth bell.' The traveller nodded. 'Eighth bell.'

And with that, the traveller entered the town whose name he still did not know.

• • • •

By eighth bell, the traveller was seated in the common room of the single inn in the small town. He'd finished a simple, but filling meal of bread and stew after a quick bath and shave. He'd changed into clean tunic and trousers and wiped the road dust from his boots. It was a matter of pride for him to be as presentable as possible this night as he felt the circumstances warranted it.

He'd ordered a pitcher of wine and a small bottle of brandy. Two wine goblets and two small glasses sat on the table but were unfilled.

At half eighth bell, the captain of the guardsmen came in. He was alone and besides the traveller and the innkeeper, who stood polishing glasses behind the bar, there were few others in the common room. The traveller's table was in the back corner, as private a spot as the common room provided.

The captain spotted him immediately and didn't hesitate to approach. His steps were measured and even, a man with a singular purpose. The traveller noted the sword at the captain's hip and shifted in his seat to adjust the sword on his own hip.

The traveller saw that the captain had changed out of his uniform into something less formal, but only just. The tunic he wore was tailored, sleeves loose around the shoulders and buttoned tight at the wrists. It was similar to the tunics the traveller also owned, designed for easy movement should things become ... less civil. His boots were polished, though well worn, and sported steel spurs on their heels. They jangled slightly with every step, but in the near empty common room, the sound was as clear as a Beltime bell being rung.

When he reached the table, the traveller stood. He saw the captain's eyes flicker down at the traveller's own sword, but he said nothing. The traveller gestured to the empty chair across from him and without a word, they both sat.

The traveller poured wine into the two goblets. He offered one to the captain, who took it but set it aside without drinking. The traveller also set his down, untasted.

They sat in silence for a long time, each taking measure of the other. Behind them, the innkeeper had ceased polishing his glasses, curiosity and a bit of concern creasing his features. After a few more moments, the traveller spoke.

'A good evening to you, Captain.'

'And to you, traveller,' the captain replied politely. 'How did you find the food here?'

'More than passable, as you suggested, especially after a long journey,' the traveller said, just as politely. 'Can I order you a meal? You must not have had time to eat after finishing your duty.'

Instead of replying to his offer, the captain asked bluntly, 'Why are you here?'

The traveller paused before answering, choosing instead to pick up his wine goblet, swirl its contents and take a small sip. It was a bit watered and tasted of berries, but as decent as he could have hoped to expect in such a small town. He took another sip as the captain sat in stony silence.

Finally, the traveller spoke. 'I'm here to share a story, to tell a tale, perhaps drink a toast.'

The captain cocked his head to one side, a note of curiosity in his voice when he said, 'What story? What tale?'

The traveller let a small smile play across his lips. 'The story of how a small act of mercy helped end a war.'

The captain leaned back, face unreadable as he studied the traveller. A few moments passed before he said quietly, 'Then tell your story, spin your tale... and we'll see about the toast.'

The traveller nodded and set his goblet down.

'This tale centres around a simple stretch of land called Greenshire. Greenshire was nothing special, held no military significance, boasted no fertile soil for crops or grass for livestock to graze upon. No, Greenshire's importance lay in the fact that it straddled the border of two kingdoms.'

The traveller paused as if in reflection. 'These two kingdoms were the greatest of the realm, with the mightiest of armies. These two kingdoms had crushed all those that had opposed them. Yet in their long, glorious, war-torn, bloody histories, these two kingdoms had never clashed with each other. Until Greenshire.'

The traveller stopped to collect himself and sipped his wine to wet his lips.

'As with all the kingdoms of this grand realm, their kings were descendants of the Immortal Dragon Lord, the First Conqueror, the Eternal Sword, the man who united this realm under one rule before shattering it to pieces. His ultimate downfall was his pride, you see. He'd married the daughters of his seven greatest warlords and sired a son upon each of those wives, a single son each, no more, and gifted each one with a dragon of their own.

'When the Conqueror decided to lay down his sword, set his crown aside, and take the Path of the Dragon, he could not decide which of his sons should rule above all others. He had grown to love each of his seven wives dearly, which proved to be a weakness. Each of those wives wanted him to favour their own son as the one true heir, as any daughter of a warlord would. They whispered poison about their sister-wives in his ear, pointed out the strengths of their own son and the weaknesses of all others. It became too much for the Conqueror to bear and so he divided the land into seven separate kingdoms with a son and dragon to rule each.

'When he had declared his intention, he was surprised and saddened that his wives and sons did not embrace his wisdom. Instead, the hate and jealousy only grew and when the Conqueror at last walked the Path, he'd left his realm to ruin.'

The traveller took a long draw from his wine to study the captain. What the traveller spoke of was what all knew, what every child had been taught, but the captain said nothing, only listened. The traveller continued.

'Once the Conqueror was truly gone, war broke out. The fathers of his seven wives mustered their armies to secure not just the kingdoms granted to each of the Conqueror's sons, their grandsons, but the kingdoms of the others. Brother crossed sword with brother and kins men were slain across the realm. The fighting became so bloody, so fierce, that the dragons of the land, weary of battling their own kind, fled the realm of Men to the mountains of the north, where no man is permitted to set foot upon penalty of death. It was at this time that the Dragon Rings were forged.

'Before departing, each of the dragons who had been gifted to the seven brothers enlisted the wizards of the land to help forge a parting gift for their former masters. They mixed their blood with that of the sons of the Conqueror into a powerful elixir and imbued it into a set of seven magical rings, one for each brother. Though they had decided to abandon the world of men, the dragons were still loyal to the one true Immortal Dragon Lord and their offspring. These rings were different from other rings of magic. They could only be worn by one with whom the blood of the Conqueror flowed. In doing so, it insured that, should one brother prove triumphant over all others, he was a true descendant of the Conqueror.

'Once the dragons disappeared into the mountains, a new war broke out. With the dragons unable to bolster their armies, the brothers faced new threats. The men of previously conquered lands rose up to reclaim their territories. Foreign armies from across the sea crossed over to try and claim dominion. Even factions within each brother's army broke away to try to carve out kingdoms of their own. It was chaos never seen since before the Conqueror united the realm.

'In the face of this anarchy, two of the Conqueror's sons forged an alliance. As their kingdoms bordered one another, they pledged to only wage war against all outside invaders, never each other. By doing so, they were able to solidify their lands through force of arms because they need never worry about an enemy at their back. As time passed, with each new generation, this alliance grew in strength. The kingdoms expanded their borders until they were the greatest in the realm. Wars still raged, but few dared to challenge the two united kingdoms. These two kingdoms bore the names of the original dragons who had been gifted to the Conqueror's sons, Tyraxia and Phrexia. '

'Then disaster struck.'

The traveller drained the last of his wine.

'Thirty years past, a dozen generations since the Time of the Conqueror, the two kings of Tyraxia and Phrexia tried to do something that no former kings of their two kingdoms had ever attempted before.' The traveller paused as if about to make a great revelation, though this was no secret. 'They tried to unite their two kingdoms into one.

'There was much debate among the great houses of each kingdom on whether this was wise or even feasible, but in the end, an agreement was struck. The much-favoured daughter of the Phrexian king would marry the equally favoured son of the Tyraxian king and that the first-born son of this royal union would rule both kingdoms. Both lands rejoiced in this announcement as the rest of the realm cursed it. Should these two kingdoms become one, no other kingdom could stand against them. It was heralded to be the beginning of a second Time of the Conqueror.

'When the time came to hold this royal marriage, the Phrexian king sent his daughter with ten thousand of his men to escort her to the Tyraxian prince for the ceremony. What neither king knew was that the Phrexian princess had already fallen in love with a Tyraxian prince... just not the one she was intended to wed. In the end, those ten thousand men were defeated by two lovesick fools and the hopes of two kingdoms were dashed when the two lovers stole away into the night. Despite an extensive search of both kingdoms where every town, hamlet and village were torn apart, they were never seen again. All agreed that the two lovers had probably crossed the sea to the continent of Khasia to disappear in its many cities.

'Naturally, both kings blamed the other for this unmitigated disaster. The disagreements grew over the years until, with much relief to the rest of the realm, all peaceful discourse ceased and the grand alliance of almost five hundred years between Tyraxia and Phrexia was no more.

'Many of the lesser lords of both kingdoms argued for a resumption of the alliance and an end to this conflict, but neither king would capitulate. Their pride and anger would not allow it.'

The captain snorted at that last statement. When the traveller lifted an eyebrow in inquiry, the captain said, 'The currency of a king's pride has always been that of a soldier's blood. And they spend it freely.'

The traveller lifted his empty goblet to the captain in agreement. 'Just so.'

The traveller took a moment to find his place in his story before resuming his tale.

'The two kings fought over everything. Slights, imagined or real, even transgressions generations past were brought to light and struggled over. But it wasn't until the Royal mapmaker of Tyraxia uncovered an ancient map of their two kingdoms that the war reached its zenith. When the ancient map had been compared to one that was deemed current, a discrepancy that gave Phrexia more land along the border between the two kingdoms was discovered. The Tyraxian king immediately demanded that the border be redrawn to correct this small discrepancy that had ceded a sliver of his land to the kingdom of Phrexia. The Phrexian king refused, of course, and so, a meaningless stretch of land far away from anything became the focal point of the war.

'A simple soldier took one look at the disputed land he would soon be fighting over and said, 'This land will become fertile with the blood we water it with.' And so, this tiny stretch of land became known to all as Greenshire.

The traveller refilled his goblet and took a long drink. His throat was dry, but, in truth, he needed a moment before continuing. The captain, sensing this, also took a small drink from his goblet before setting it down again. The traveller took a deep breath and resumed speaking.

'The two kings mustered their armies and marched day and night towards Greenshire. The Tyraxian army was led by the very son that had been jilted by the Phrexian princess while the Phrexian forces were led by the last trueborn child of the Phrexian king, the Prince Heir.

'Both princes had been popular amongst their people, and each carried the hope of their nations for a decisive victory and an end to this destructive conflict. In total, over two hundred thousand soldiers marched on Greenshire.'

The traveller closed his eyes. He could still see the endless waves of men that stretched for miles. He recalled the cloud of dust that rose in the army's wake to almost blot out the sun. At first, it had been a glorious sight to behold, but now, it only filled him with grief and sadness for how few of those men returned home.

'Most wars fought in open ground are decided in a day, perhaps as many as three, before a victor claims triumph. The War for Greenshire lasted almost a fortnight.

'The two princes were master tacticians, orchestrating their own attacks with precision and countering their opponents with skill, so that for the first seven days, the two armies fought to a standstill, neither being able to say they bested the other. However, the war took a marked turn when the Tyraxian prince was struck down and grievously wounded.

'It happened when a small force of Phrexian cavalry broke through the Tyraxian lines to reach the prince. The Phrexians slew his guard to the man, as well as the rest of the Tyraxian military commanders. The prince, a skilled warrior in his own right, was able to fight them off for a time, but it became certain that their numbers would overwhelm him before help could rally to his aid. It was then that a lone Tyraxian soldier, a captain, who had fought to his side, cast himself between the Phrexian forces and his prince with naught else but a sword and shield. This lone soldier planted his feet over his fallen prince and held. He took blow after blow on his shield but would not yield. He swung his sword until he could lift it no longer and, still, he would not be defeated. He held until he could hold no longer, but it was just long enough for Tyraxian reinforcements to arrive and beat back the attacking Phrexians.

'The prince was rushed from the battlefield where they were able to treat his wounds and preserve his life. When he could speak, the prince called for the captain who had saved his life. It turned out that this young captain was not unknown to the prince. This captain had been fostered at the home of the prince's uncle, a renowned general that was known across the realm simply as The Redwood. The prince knew that his uncle had tutored and trained the captain in the art of war and that, with his military commanders all slain, he would need that knowledge and training if the Tyraxians had any hope of being victorious. So, on the eighth day of the War for Greenshire, the Tyraxian prince made a young captain, landless and of no noble birth, the Warlord to the Tyraxian army and bid him to win the war.

'At first, the other commanders questioned the orders of this young Warlord as he changed the tactics they had previously employed, not believing him seasoned enough to make such decisions. But as the war continued and his battle plans led to victory after victory, the questions and doubts ceased and they began to refer to him as they did the prince's uncle, as The Redwood.'

The captain cocked his head to one side, eyebrows lifted. 'So, it was the protege that took over and not that old battle-axe?'

The traveller smiled. 'Yes, the real Redwood had retired after the death of his wife to raise their daughter as he could not bear the thought of being separated from her to grow up alone.'

The captain nodded as if this explanation made perfect sense and motioned for the traveller to continue.

'The young captain turned Warlord, at first resisted this new moniker, but gave over once he realized that the Tyraxian men would rally more for someone called The Redwood instead of an unknown and untried captain whom they had never heard of.

'Not only that, but this new Redwood fought alongside his men where the fighting was fiercest, never hesitating to engage the enemy Phrexians even when it looked likely that the Tyraxians would meet defeat. And the men loved him for it.

'What they didn't know was that this new Warlord struggled with his new command, his new responsibilities. Never before had any of his previous orders as a mere captain resulted in the death of so many men. It weighed on him when the rosters of the fallen were brought to him at the end of the day. He'd read name after name of the dead, friends and comrades alike, long into the night and, even when exhaustion at last took him, he could find no rest. By the eighteenth day of Greenshire, the young Warlord felt he had aged a dozen years.'

The captain, when the traveller paused, quietly said, 'It is no easy task to bear such a burden, the lives of other men.'

The traveller didn't respond, save to take another drink of his wine.

The traveller continued. 'On the morning of the nineteenth day, the Warlord was once again in the thick of battle. They had whittled away at the Phrexian forces, and it seemed that a Tyraxian victory was all but assured if they could but just take the day. It was then that he saw a sad sight that nearly broke him.'

The traveller set aside his empty wine goblet. The wine, even watered, had begun to go to his head and he wanted to remain as alert as possible.

The traveller continued on. 'When the army of Tyraxia first mustered, the king's military advisors warned him that Phrexia's numbers were too great to be overcome. They begged him for more men from the outlying border outposts to bolster their own forces. However, the outposts had already sent every spare man and losing any more would jeopardize the security of the border. Every available mercenary force was engaged until the treasury was all but depleted. He even considered treaties with the other neighbouring territories for men before discarding it as too risky. So, the King sent out heralds to every corner of the kingdom seeking volunteers.

'At first, every able-bodied man flocked to the King's banner. Farmers, craftsmen, merchants, retired soldiers and more came to fight, but it still wasn't enough. So, with all other options exhausted, the King instituted a new law of conscription. All unmarried men who had reached their majority were conscripted into the army. Any family with two sons would have to send the eldest if they had reached at least their fifteenth summer. It was an unpopular act that caused dissension throughout the kingdom, but the King finally had the numbers he felt he needed to win the war.

'What he didn't understand was that these conscripts had never bore arms or received any kind of military training. So, they were given rudimentary instructions, whatever weapon was handy and, if they were lucky, bits of armour, a helmet, maybe a shield, and told to march to war. 'On the march, many of the seasoned soldiers, including the young captain, did what they could to train and drill them in the use of their arms and the most basic of military manoeuvres. They did their best, but there simply wasn't enough time to make them more than a step above competent before they reached Greenshire.

'Prior to the young Warlord taking over command, the conscripts were used as no more than fodder against the Phrexian infantry with the hopes that their numbers would overwhelm a superiorly trained opponent.' The traveller paused, his voice now bleak. 'Their losses were terrible.'

The traveller fell silent. He knew that the captain, as a soldier, would understand the depth of the grief he felt for how callously the lives of those conscripts were thrown away.

'One of the first things the Warlord ordered upon his promotion was the dispersion of the remaining conscripts to more veteran units. Every unit had taken losses and replacements were sorely needed, even ones as unseasoned as the conscripts. Even so, there were still whole companies of conscripts that were kept together. It was one of these units that became the focal point of a Phrexian charge of cavalry.'

The traveller took a breath and closed his eyes, lost in the memory. The captain said nothing, only waited.

'The commander of the Phrexian cavalry had learned to identity weak spots in the Tyraxian line and attacked the company of conscripts, thinking that it couldn't stand against his charge. The Warlord, as was his wont, was patrolling the battle, sending orders, when he saw the cavalry make its charge. He mobilized his troops to reinforce the conscripts, but he believed that he would be too late.

'Yet, against all odds, the conscripts held,' the traveller said, a touch of wonder entering his voice. 'They were being slaughtered, and still, in the face of death and certain defeat, they stood tall.'

The captain shifted in his seat, an unreadable expression on his weathered face. The traveller thought that he even saw a slight smile crack his otherwise stony visage.

'The conscripts somehow knew that if those cavalrymen got behind their lines, the entire Tyraxian battlefront would collapse. They knew that if they broke through, that the day would be lost. So, they held.

'It was a sight to behold for the young Warlord. He'd never witnessed such bravery in soldiers so untrained. The company had men too old by far and others too young by half to ever fight in a war, yet they spent their lives in reckless abandon. They threw themselves beneath the charging horses, hoping to make them trip, stumble or slow them down long enough to pull their riders from their saddles. They swarmed riders even as they were cut down with sword, spear or hoof. Even as they died, they screamed defiance with their last breath. And they held.

'The Warlord arrived with the reinforcements just as the last of them were brought down, but the charge was foiled. It was at that moment the Warlord saw a thing that would help change the course of the war for both Tyraxia and Phrexia.

'Just at the edge of the battle, too far for the Warlord to reach in time, stood a lone conscript, perhaps the last one still alive or not mortally wounded. It was a young lad, battered and bloody, standing over the bodies of his fallen comrades. He held naught but a broken spear gripped in his fist and a shattered shield strapped to his arm, but he stood defiantly, ready to give his life for Tyraxia. Before him was a single Phrexian cavalryman, sword raised, ready to strike him down. This cavalryman had lost his helmet, face bloody from a wound, but his eyes were clear as he made ready to finish this young conscript off.'

The traveller paused as the captain shifted in his seat. The traveller's eyes flickered to the scar on the captain's face but didn't linger.

'However,' the traveller said, continuing his tale, 'the blow never fell. Instead, in the midst of all those bodies, both Tyraxian and Phrexian, that cavalryman stayed his sword and let the conscript live. Then, lifting his sword in salute, the cavalryman wheeled his mount away and quit the field. To this day, the Warlord never knew for certain why he did this. Why, after eighteen days of war, this Phrexian performed this one act of mercy.'

The traveller said nothing for a long moment. The captain, likewise, was silent. Instead, they regarded each other across the table, an air of expectation simmering between them.

It was the captain who broke the stalemate, offering up, 'Perhaps, he was tired and wounded and knew that the attack had failed.'

The traveller cocked his head to one side in contemplation. 'Perhaps,' he said. 'Or maybe the cavalryman was tired of the blood and battle.'

The captain snorted in derision. 'Soldiers fight. They die. This is the risk they take, the fate they may suffer at any moment when they go to war.'

The traveller nodded. 'Just so,' he said. 'Then why spare the lad if this was his moment? Why not finish off one more of the enemy? Why let him live?'

The captain gave the traveller an angry glare. 'Who can say? Perhaps that Phrexian didn't know either. Perhaps, as you say, he decided that he'd killed enough that day. Perhaps he was too wounded to be sure of his sword,' he said. 'Many soldiers in the heat of battle will do things that even they can't comprehend, much less anyone else.'

'Perhaps,' the traveller agreed. 'But I don't think so in this instance.'

The captain looked away; jaw clenched. 'No, you are right. I think that when the cavalryman looked down upon this lad in his tattered uniform, gripping that broken spear and shield, with that look of foolhardy courage on his bloody face, he reminded him of someone else.

Another lad with foolhardy courage, perhaps, that he had lost in another battle, another war. A lad who only wanted to make his father proud and ended up dying a meaningless death, breaking his father's heart. Perhaps, he saw another son of a father and couldn't bear to be the one to strike him down.'

The captain fell silent, eyes wet with unshed tears as the traveller looked on in sympathy.

They both heard a sound, a muffled sob. As one, they turned to survey the common room and saw that a small crowd had collected behind them. There were the guardsmen from the gatehouse mingled in with some of the townsfolk, all sitting or standing at the tables. Both men, lost in the telling and listening of the tale, hadn't known so many had gathered to listen. Yet, they all watched the pair, none making a sound. Their faces were a mixture of sadness and rapt attention at the words being spoken. The guardsman the traveller had saluted sat alone, tears unabashedly streaming down his face, a soldier perhaps with his own sad tale. Even the too eager guardsman, Layton, sat at a table, eyes solemn as he squeezed the hand of a pretty young woman leaning against his shoulder, belly round with child. Her other hand moved up and down, stroking his arm in comfort.

The captain turned back around, grabbed his wine goblet and drained it. The traveller refilled it without asking.

'His name was Rory,' the traveller said.

'What?'

'The lad that had been spared. His name was Rory,' the traveller answered. 'After the two forces had broken apart for the day to regroup, treat their wounded and collect their dead, the Warlord had him sought out. Why, the Warlord could not say for sure, except that he wanted to meet him, to hear his tale. I think he felt a certain responsibility for him, an obligation he needed to meet.

'When he was brought to his tent that night, the lad was quaking with fear, thinking he had done some wrong to be summoned to the

Warlord's private tent. But the Warlord only praised him for his courage and that of his comrades. You would have laughed to see how far his chest had puffed out in pride at the Warlord's words. The Warlord bade him to sit down, share his meal with him and tell his tale.'

The traveller smiled sadly as he continued to speak. If he was conscious of the crowd now listening, he didn't allow it to show, as his tale wasn't for them. 'It turns out that Rory was the son of a scribe from a small village on the far edge of Tyraxia called Coldbrook. It was called that, Rory had said, for no other reason than it had been built next to a small stream. His family had been the village scribes for as long as Coldbrook had existed, and his father had already taken his son as apprentice to carry on the family profession.'

The traveller went on. 'The thing is, that son hadn't been Rory. No, Rory was actually the second son, two years younger than his brother, Lucas.'

The captain looked up at that, eyebrows raised. 'Second son?'

The traveller nodded. 'You see, when the law of conscription was put down, it should have been Lucas who was sent to war, not Rory, as Rory was only fourteen summers old.'

'Fourteen?' the captain gasped in disbelief. 'Gods!'

The traveller nodded in agreement. 'The Warlord was as shocked as you were that any father would send a lad of fourteen to war. He was furious with Rory's father and vowed to bring him to account, but Rory had said no. Instead, he calmly told the Warlord that he had volunteered in Lucas's stead, that his parents had no idea he had done so until the conscription wagon had left Coldbrook.

'Why would you do this, the Warlord had asked. And Rory had told him that Lucas was, as their father's apprentice, the favoured son and that both parents had doted on him. Rory was in no way neglected, but he simply wasn't Lucas. Lucas was funny, clever and dutiful, while Rory was dull and possessed no head for the learning of letters needed to be a scribe. His parents had wept when the conscription law was announced as much for believing their son was going to war as being left with Rory as the new apprentice.

'So, when the wagon came to round up the village's conscripts, Rory had already conspired with another friend being conscripted to lock Lucas in his family's cellar. Lucas was furious, of course, as he loved Rory far more than his parents ever did, being the dutiful brother as well as son. However, Lucas was slight of frame and though two summers younger, Rory was already taller and stronger than Lucas, and Rory and his friend were easily able to overpower him. When the conscripts arrived, they, given how big he was for his age, took Rory without question when he put himself forth as his family's required conscript. So, Rory made his mark and left Coldbrook behind forever, his parents none the wiser.

'The Warlord asked Rory if he had at least left his parents a note explaining, but Rory had said no. Why ever not, the Warlord had asked, and Rory's answer had made his heart shatter. I didn't leave a note or tell them, Rory had replied, because I don't think I could have borne it if they hadn't tried to stop me.'

With that, the traveller looked down in sadness, thinking of how awful it would be to believe that your parents didn't love you enough to want to keep you. The captain said nothing.

The traveller went on. 'The Warlord then made a decision. He appointed Rory as his personal bannerman to carry his banner into battle. By Rory's reaction, you would have thought that he had been offered the world. The Warlord, over the course of the evening, had grown fond of this brave young lad of fourteen summers from Coldbrook who had stood down the charge of a Phrexian cavalryman with nothing but a broken spear and shield. The Warlord wanted to keep him safe and away from the worst of the fighting and believed that this was the best way to do so. What a fool that Warlord was.'

The captain closed his eyes. He spoke without opening them.

'So, he is gone.'

The traveller's silence was confirmation enough without words, as no words could be spoken for this.

'How?' the captain rasped; voice hoarse with emotion.

'On the nineteenth day of the war for Greenshire, the Warlord took to the battlefield, surrounded by his guard and new bannerman. He'd charged Rory to under no circumstances, engage in battle, that his sole task and duty was to hold the Warlord's banner high for all his troops to see. That way, the Warlord believed, he would be in less danger.'

The traveller took a breath before going on. 'But the Warlord didn't take into account Rory's heart, his foolhardy bravery. And when a small coterie of Phrexian soldiers spied the Warlord's banner, they staged a reckless assault to bring down the Warlord of the Tyraxian army once and for all. The Warlord was quickly surrounded, his guard overwhelmed. And while the Warlord was fighting off two soldiers, a third came at him from behind, poised to strike him down with a spear. As the Phrexian soldier thrust his spear at the Warlord, it was then that Rory cast himself between them and took that fatal strike through his own chest, grasping the spear shaft, even as he fell, so that there could be no second attempt, giving his life without a second thought to save that of the Warlord's.'

The traveller stopped, took a breath.

'The Warlord didn't remember what happened next. Later, his men told him that he seemed to go mad, crazed with bloodlust. That he slew every Phrexian soldier around him until the rest had fled, unable to withstand his fury. Afterwards, they found him cradling the body of his young bannerman amidst a pile of the dead, weeping.'

The captain stared at the traveller for a long breath. Then he lifted the wine pitcher to fill the traveller's empty goblet. The traveller nodded his thanks and took a long drink.

'That night, the Warlord sent a herald to the Phrexian prince that he wanted to parlay on the morrow. And so, on the twentieth day of the battle for Greenshire, the Tyraxian Warlord and the Phrexian prince met alone in the centre of the battlefield under a flag of truce to speak of ending the war.

'Military advisors and commanders argued against this meeting for different reasons. The Tyraxians believed that the war was all but won, that a final push was all that was needed to crush the Phrexian army. Meanwhile, the Phrexians believed that nothing could be gained through diplomacy and that the Tyraxians were certain only to demand terms of surrender that would leave the prince in disgrace. But this was not the case.

'The Warlord, sick with grief over Rory's death and the death of so many other Tyraxians, just wanted an end to the war. The Phrexian prince, surprisingly, was of the same mind. Of the two thousand combined soldiers from both kingdoms that had marched on Greenshire, less than ten thousand had survived. It was as destructive a single conflict as ever in the history of the realm, much less either kingdom. An entire generation of soldiers had been lost and both kingdoms weakened beyond measure.

'The Warlord knew that the Tyraxian prince would never agree to anything less than total victory, if for no other reason than to soothe his injured pride. The Phrexian prince, likewise, knew that he could never return to his father, the King, without the same result, so they came to a compromise. The two men, Warlord and Prince, were accomplished soldiers, neither sure if one of them was a more capable warrior than the other. So, they agreed to a duel. A duel to the death to decide the fate of Greenshire and the war. The winner would claim victory, but both armies would withdraw from the field regardless of the outcome. They had decided, that, beyond this final duel, there would be no more fighting, no more Tyraxian or Phrexian soldiers dying over a meaningless stretch of land. One death to prevent ten thousand more.'

'Before leaving the parlay tent, the two men, Warlord and prince, embraced like brothers. One of them would slay the other in only a little while, but in that moment, they were allies in the common cause of peace.'

The traveller looked up at the crowd gathered in the common room of the inn. He had been speaking for well over an hour, but none of his audience showed any sign of wanting to leave. Even the innkeeper had abandoned his bar to perch on a stool in the corner. Their eyes met and the innkeeper gave him a small nod to continue, though it must have been long past closing for the inn. The traveller spoke on.

'Upon returning to the Tyraxian camp, the Warlord gave orders that his commanders didn't understand. 'Prepare to withdraw? ' they asked again and again, unsure if they had heard correctly. 'Yes', the Warlord responded, 'those are my orders. In one hours time, I will meet the Phrexian prince in combat to decide the war, but no matter what, we withdraw. No more Tyraxian blood will be spilled, or lives lost today, save perhaps my own.'

'The commanders all protested, of course, but they obeyed and the Tyraxians broke their war camp for the long march home. On the Phrexian side of the battlefield, similar preparations were taking place and when the Tyraxian soldiers saw this, they let out a cheer. Most didn't understand what was taking place or why their Phrexian counterparts were cheering just as loudly, save for one thing: the war was over for them.

'When the Warlord emerged from his tent, armour and shield cleaned and polished to a bright sheen, sword buckled at his waist, his soldiers cheered twice as loud as before. Word of the duel had spread quickly and all preparations to leave ceased so that they could bear witness. As the Warlord began to make his way to the appointed spot, the cheering abruptly died down so quickly that the Warlord was momentarily confused at the silence. But what he saw made his heart swell with pride and gratitude. The Tyraxian soldiers, his soldiers, to a man, were lined up in formation and standing at attention and as he passed his brave warriors, they all raised their swords and spears in salute. So many had perished under his command that the Warlord had been certain that they despised him and cursed the day he was given command, but it was not so. The Warlord vowed to himself that he would not fail them as he had failed Rory. That, even should he fall, he would honour them with his life as they had honoured him with theirs.

'At the edge of the spot that he and the prince had agreed upon, the Warlord stopped. He himself stood at attention, turned smartly on his heel to face the Tyraxian camp, drew his sword and raised it high in salute to his men. The resounding roar that crashed down upon him, cheers and banging of weapons upon shield or earth, buoyed his spirit and brought tears to his eyes. The Warlord was now ready to end this war, one way or another.

'The Phrexian prince already stood waiting for him. Resplendent in his own shining armour and shield, the prince was flanked by his honour guard, the Red Maidens. All fierce, highly trained warriors in their own right, the Red Maidens existed for a singular purpose, to protect the royal line of Phrexia. The Warlord could see how upset they were that this duel was happening, and half expected them to bundle the prince up and whisk him away. But when the prince sent them off, they reluctantly obeyed. Behind the prince, the Phrexian army stood, watching in silence. When the prince turned to his army and saluted them as the Warlord had to his own men, the resulting roar was as loud as the Tyraxians' had been. The two men, Warlord and prince, then met in the middle of the clearing.'

'Let us put an end to this, Tyraxian', the prince said.

'I am ready, Phrexian', the Warlord replied.

A murmur went up from the listening crowd in the room. The traveller let a small smile find his lips as he acknowledged their muted enthusiasm for his tale. Even the captain was leaning forward slightly, eager to hear more.

'They each stepped back and made their final prayers to their gods. For the Warlord, it was Tares, Earth Goddess of War. As he had done every day since coming to Greenshire, the Warlord cut his hand on his sword and knelt to press it flat against the earth, an offering of blood to Tares for Her blessing in battle. The cut healed, his offering accepted, Her blessing granted.

'When the Warlord stood, the prince was still on one knee, speaking softly in prayer, head bowed over the pommel of his sword, point driven into the earth. The Warlord didn't know what gods the Phrexian prince worshipped, but he waited for him to finish out of honour and respect.'

'Lashia,' the captain interjected.

'What's that?' the traveller asked.

'Lashia, Goddess of Death and Rebirth,' the captain explained. 'That is who this Phrexian prince worshipped.'

The traveller made a small gesture of thanks to the captain for his words and knowledge before continuing his tale.

'When the prince stood, the two men saluted one another one last time. There were no more words to be spoken, nothing further to be said.

'They rushed forward, and the battle was begun. Their swords flashed back and forth, ringing with every clash of their blades. Both armies stood in silence so that the sound of their struggle echoed across the battlefield. So evenly matched were they, that neither could breach the other's defences. These two master swordsmen danced back and forth, each gaining ground before ceding it back just as swiftly. Soon, they were both heaving in exhaustion, sweat coursing down their faces from their exertions and heat from the sun. They broke apart long enough to cast their helmets aside to wipe their eyes free of sweat before resuming the duel.

'The prince drew first blood, scoring a strike inside the Warlord's shield along his left hip with a sudden thrust that if a few inches further in, would have crippled the Warlord, ending it then and there. When the Warlord staggered back, the Phrexian army threw up a cheer in support of their prince while the Tyraxian army grew quiet with dread. But the Warlord would not be denied.

'Faking how severe the injury was, the Warlord slowed his movements, pretending to favour his injured side. The prince may or may not have been fooled, but he took the bait, nonetheless.'

The crowd in the inn collectively groaned, anticipating the traveller's next words.

'The prince renewed his assault on the Warlord, focusing his attack on his injured side. But the Warlord was only biding his time, waiting for an opening in the prince's defence, and, when the prince swung his sword next, he overextended himself and the Warlord ran him through.'

The captain let out a sigh of resignation. 'He always was too eager for that finishing blow.'

The traveller merely shrugged, choosing not to respond to the captain's comment.

'The end was so sudden that, at first, the two armies were stunned into silence. Then, as the Warlord withdrew his sword from his honoured opponent's body and gently lowered the dying prince to the ground, the Tyraxian army exploded in celebration. In contrast, the Phrexian army roared, beating their shields in fury. So intense was their anger that the Warlord feared that they would charge across the battlefield and the fighting would begin anew, negating their prince's sacrifice.

'But they held their place and the Warlord turned to his own army and raised his arms in a placating gesture, not wanting them to incite the Phrexians further. After a long moment, the cheering died down and there was silence once more on the battlefield.

'The Warlord bent over the body of the Phrexian prince, gripping his hand until the prince breathed his last and his hand fell limp from the Warlord's grasp. The prince had not tried to speak at the end, simply allowing his eyes to close, a serene expression on his face. A quiet end to an honourable man and a noble prince.'

'The traveller bowed his head in remembrance of the Phrexian prince's death. The common room, likewise, was also respectfully silent. The captain's eyes were shut, lips moving in what the traveller believed was a quiet prayer to either Lashia or his own god of worship. The traveller waited until he finished to conclude his tale.

'The Warlord picked up the prince's fallen sword. It was a fine sword of good steel, but not fancy or ornate as one might expect a prince's sword to be. It was a soldiers sword, well used and equally well cared for. It made the Warlord respect the prince that much more for possessing it, much less wielding it in their duel. The Warlord laid the sword lengthwise on the prince's body and folded the prince's hands over the swords hilt. The Warlord wanted the prince to have his sword in the afterlife, armed to the last. The Warlord stood and pressing his fist to his heart, honoured the prince with a final salute.

'When he turned, the Warlord realized that he was surrounded by a half dozen of the prince's guard, the Red Maidens. He thought they meant to have their vengeance on him, but he was wrong. All but one of them were weeping silently over their fallen charge as they ignored his slayer. The Red Maidens didn't speak, but, as one, they lifted the prince's body onto a litter, their touch light and gentle, so as not to disturb his sword, and bore him back to the Phrexian camp. As they approached the line of Phrexian soldiers, they parted to allow them through, many falling to their knees in grief. When they passed through, the army closed behind the Red Maidens, and they disappeared from the Warlord's sight with their solemn burden.

'The Warlord, exhausted and wounded, faced the Phrexian army one last time. He saluted them as he would any other worthy opponent, raising his sword to show his respect. The Phrexian's, in response, returned the gesture with sword and spear. Then, the Warlord turned away and departed the battlefield, leaving behind Greenshire and those countless fallen soldiers behind forever.

'So concludes the tale of how a single act of mercy helped bring about the end of the War for Greenshire and a reforging of the alliance between Tyraxia and Phrexia.'

There was a smattering of applause from the common room and even the captain tapped the table with his palm in appreciation.

'A well told tale, traveller,' the captain said.

The traveller nodded his head in thanks.

'Yeah, but is it all true?' the too eager guard, Layton, asked, eyes narrowed in mistrust. 'All that stuff about the cavalryman and that lad.'

The woman at his side tried to shush him, but he waved her off, his expression demanding an answer. The rest of the crowd seemed to be waiting for a response as well, so the traveller decided to oblige them.

'All tales have truth, as well as lies, depending on who tells it and who listens,' the traveller said with a slight smile.

'What kind an answer is it?' Layton scoffed. 'Is it true or ain't it?'

This time, it was the captain who answered. 'It's true enough,' he said, giving Layton a long look.

'Aye,' the other guardsman, the one who had been weeping, concurred. 'True enough.'

With that, the crowd dispersed, some going to their rooms in the inn while the remainder filed out the door to return to their homes. Layton, hand in hand with the pregnant woman the traveller assumed was his wife, and the other guardsman were the last to depart. As he was about to leave, the guardsman paused long enough to salute the traveller one last time, fist to heart. The traveller returned the gesture and with a final nod, the guardsman left.

· · · ·

With the common room all but empty, the innkeeper began to clean and wipe the vacated tables, careful to steer clear of the table where the traveller and captain still sat.

'One final drink, captain, before you go?' the traveller asked, reaching for the bottle of brandy and two glasses.

The captain didn't answer. He was staring at the wall, face lost in thought or, perhaps, dwelling on past memories. He was silent for so long that the traveller prompted him again. 'Captain?'

The captain turned to face the traveller and looked him in the eye. 'I know who you are,' he said quietly.

The traveller leaned back in his chair with a sigh, leaving the brandy bottle and glasses untouched. He returned the captain's look with one of his own. 'And I you.'

The captain nodded, face grim. 'I recognized you the moment you appeared at the gatehouse.'

'And I you,' the traveller repeated.

The captain blew out a frustrated breath. 'Why come here?' he demanded, genuine bewilderment in his voice. 'Why come to Phrexia where every hand would be against you? And, of all places, why here?'

The traveller shrugged. 'As I said before, I was looking for a man so I could share a tale and,' gesturing to the untouched brandy, 'perhaps a drink. I found the man, shared my tale and now, I would be most honoured to share that drink.'

The captain looked away, shaking his head. 'Why would I share a drink with you?' he finally inquired, a touch of malice in his tone.

'To allow me to thank you,' the traveller said simply.

'To thank me?' the captain said in astonishment. 'For what am I owed thanks? Sparing a boy's life so he could save yours so, you, in turn, could kill my prince? Thanks for that? You must be mad!'

The traveller grinned, amused at the captain's reaction and, perhaps, a bit at himself. 'I have been called mad before,' he said. 'And I should have expected you to think as you do, but some things are never as simple as one views them, Captain. You should know that better than most.'

The Captain responded with an angry glare.

The traveller sighed. 'All that you said is true,' he conceded. 'But it is also true that your single act of mercy did more than that. It granted me three gifts, all of which I am equally grateful for.'

When the captain said nothing, the traveller went on. 'The first gift was that of Rory. Even for so brief a time as I had him, he meant a great deal to me and not just for saving my life, such as it is. The second gift was that by meeting Rory, then losing him, you helped grant me the clarity of vision to consider the possibility of finding a way to end the war, even though it cost you your prince. And the last gift, the most important one of all, is one that all of Tyraxia and Phrexia should be thanking you for. With the end of the war, you helped saved the lives of over ten thousand men... fathers, sons, brothers... all who were able to return home when so many could not. And not just that, but it also opened the door to peace between our two kingdoms, even a peace as tenuous as this one is. So, again, I say, thank you.'

With that, the traveller took up the bottle of brandy and poured. When both glasses were filled, he slid one across the table towards the captain.

The captain stared at the glass for so long that the traveller believed he would leave it untouched. Or pick it up only to empty its contents on the floor... or in the traveller's face. But, in the end, the captain reached out and gingerly lifted it up, a look of consideration on his face. He studied the glass for another moment, perhaps seeing more than just brandy in its contents.

'Very well,' the captain said gruffly. 'One drink.'

The traveller smiled in gratitude. 'One drink,' he said.

The captain said, 'To my prince, may his sacrifice not be in vain.'

The traveller said, 'To the end of the war for Greenshire, may we never see it's like again.'

The captain replied, 'To all our fallen comrades, may they ever find eternal peace.'

The traveller nodded before adding quietly, 'To acts of mercy, may they always offer hope to whoever receives them.'

The traveller and captain shared a long look and, as one, said, 'To Rory.'

Then, the two men, traveller and captain, Warlord and cavalryman, Tyraxian and Phrexian, touched glasses and drank.

# Don't miss out!

Visit the website below and you can sign up to receive emails whenever S J Parker publishes a new book. There's no charge and no obligation.

https://books2read.com/r/B-A-RLVZ-MDTMC

BOOKS 2 READ

Connecting independent readers to independent writers.

# About the Author

S J Parker is currently a resident of Arizona, USA, where he continues to work on his personal growth.

He can be contacted through his publisher via email at - talesfromdeathrow@gmail.com

# About the Publisher

This book has been published by S J Parker's wife. Together they compiled his writing into this collection of short stories and poetry.

They have been a couple since 2019 and married in 2023. She currently lives in the UK and visits Arizona regularly.

www.ingramcontent.com/pod-product-compliance
Lightning Source LLC
Chambersburg PA
CBHW051250160726
47994CB00003B/1101